WHO LEADS OUR COUNTRY?

By Jacqueline Laks Gorman
Reading consultant: Susan Nations, M.Ed.,
author/literacy coach/consultant in literacy development

WEEKLY READER
PUBLISHING

Please visit our web site at www.garethstevens.com
For a free color catalog describing our list of high-quality books,
call 1-800-542-2595 (USA) or 1-800-387-3178 (Canada). Our fax: 1-877-542-2596

Library of Congress Cataloging-in-Publication Data

Gorman, Jacqueline Laks, 1955-
    Who leads our country? / Jacqueline Laks Gorman.
       p. cm. — (Know your government)
    Includes index.
    ISBN-13: 978-0-8368-8841-6 (lib. bdg.)
    ISBN-10: 0-8368-8841-3 (lib. bdg.)
    ISBN-13: 978-0-8368-8846-1 (softcover)
    ISBN-10: 0-8368-8846-4 (softcover)
    1. Political leadership—United States—Juvenile literature. 2. United States—
Politics and government—Decision making—Juvenile literature. I. Title.
JK1726.G66   2008
320.473—dc22   2007027917

This edition first published in 2008 by
Weekly Reader® Books
An Imprint of Gareth Stevens Publishing
1 Reader's Digest Road
Pleasantville, NY 10570-7000 USA

Copyright © 2008 by Gareth Stevens, Inc.

Senior Editor: Brian Fitzgerald
Creative Director: Lisa Donovan
Senior Designer: Keith Plechaty
Layout: Cynthia Malaran
Photo Research: Charlene Pinckney and Kimberly Babbitt

Photo credits: cover & title page Olga Bogatyrenko/Shutterstock, p. 5 Dave Huss/PhotoSpin; p. 7 William
Vasta/AP/The White House; p. 8 Pablo Martinez Monsivais/AP; p. 9 Jim Watson/AFP/Getty Images;
p. 10 Gerald Herbert/AP; p. 12 Weekly Reader Archives; p. 13 Courtesy, Office of the Speaker;
p. 15 © Nick Ut/Pool/Corbis; p. 16 Erik S. Lesser/Getty Images; p. 17 © Dana White/PhotoEdit;
p. 19 Photograph by Steve Petteway, Collection of the Supreme Court of the U.S.; p. 20 © Spencer Grant/
PhotoEdit; p. 21 Jim Watson/AFP/Getty Images

Printed in the United States of America

1 2 3 4 5 6 7 8 9 10 09 08 07

TABLE OF CONTENTS

Words that appear in the glossary are printed in **boldface** type the first time they appear in the text.

CHAPTER 1

A Nation With Many Leaders

Every February, the United States celebrates Presidents' Day. We honor two presidents who were born in February. They are George Washington and Abraham Lincoln. We also honor all the other presidents on that day. The president is the leader of the United States.

The president lives and works in the White House in Washington, D.C.

The president is not our only government leader. Many men and women act as leaders in the United States. Some work in Washington, D.C., the country's capital. Other leaders work in states, cities, or towns. We need good leaders to help keep people safe and free.

CHAPTER 2

What Does the President Do?

The president has one of the hardest jobs in the world. The president has to decide what is best for the country. Sometimes the president has to lead the country during times of trouble.

The president works for all Americans. Voters **elect,** or choose, a president every four years. A person can be elected president only two times. The president has many different duties.

Chief Executive

The president is the country's chief executive. The president works closely with Congress. Congress is the part of government that makes laws. The president makes sure that laws are carried out.

A **bill** is a written idea for a new law. The president has to approve a bill before it becomes a law. The president can also give Congress ideas for new laws.

In 1997, President Bill Clinton signed a bill into law. The new law helped protect children.

The president oversees all government departments. The president chooses men and women to lead these departments. There are government departments for health, education, and other important areas. The heads of these departments work with the president. Together they try to solve problems in the country.

In July 2007, President George W. Bush met with his top advisers to talk about the war in Iraq.

In February 2006, President Bush met with Ellen Johnson-Sirleaf. She is the president of Liberia, a country in Africa.

Commander-in-Chief

The president is in charge of the **military.** The military includes the Army, Navy, Air Force, and Marines. The military protects the country. Sometimes the president sends the military into battle. Congress must approve this action.

World Leader

The president is also a leader in the world. The president meets with leaders from other countries. They work together to help solve problems.

9

President Bush honored Peyton Manning (left) and the rest of the Indianapolis Colts for winning the Super Bowl in 2007.

Head of State

The president is a symbol of our country. The president sometimes goes on television to tell Americans how the country is doing. The president also honors important people. Community leaders, athletes, and children may visit the president at the White House.

CHAPTER 3

What Does Congress Do?

Congress has two parts. Those parts are the Senate and the House of Representatives. Congress makes the laws for our country.

Each state elects members of Congress. There are 100 **senators.** Each of the fifty states has two senators. There are 435 **representatives.** The number of representatives from a state depends on the number of people who live there.

Any member of Congress can suggest a bill for a new law. The Senate and the House vote on the bill. The bill passes if most members vote for it. To become a law, the bill must be approved by the president. The president may not agree with the bill. The bill can still become a law if two-thirds of both the Senate and the House vote for it.

Members of Congress work in the Capitol building in Washington, D.C.

Congress decides how the government should spend its money. Every year, Congress prepares a **budget.** The budget is a plan for how much money the government will spend.

Congress helps solve problems in the country. Members of Congress also visit their home states often. They talk to the people they represent and find out what those people need.

In July 2007, Congresswoman Nancy Pelosi spoke to people from her home state of California.

CHAPTER 4

What Do Governors and Mayors Do?

Each state has its own government. The **governor** is the head of the state government. The people in the state elect the governor. Each state has a **legislature.** This group of people passes new state laws. The governor must sign a bill before it can become a state law. Then the governor sees that the law is followed.

Governor Arnold Schwarzenegger of California thanked firefighters who helped out after an earthquake struck in 2003.

Governors pick many of the people who help run the state. The state government keeps law and order. It helps keep the roads safe and helps run the schools. Governors and the state legislature work together to decide how to spend the state's money. The governor also helps the people in the state during an emergency.

Shirley Franklin was elected mayor of Atlanta, Georgia, in 2002. She was the city's first female African American mayor.

The United States has many cities and towns. Each has its own government. **Mayors** are the government leaders in many of these places. The mayor is elected by the people in the city or town. He or she makes sure the city or town runs smoothly.

Many cities and towns have **councils.** The people in the community elect the members of the council. The mayor works with the council. The council passes laws to make the community a better place to live. The city or town government may run the schools, libraries, and parks.

City council members often hold meetings. They listen to people from their community talk about important issues.

CHAPTER 5

What Do Courts Do?

People settle disagreements about the law in court. Judges are leaders of the courts. They make sure that everyone is treated fairly under the law.

The Supreme Court is the top court in the United States. The president picks the judges, called justices, for the Court. The Senate must approve the president's choices. The Supreme Court decides whether the laws passed by Congress and by state governments are fair.

The U.S. Supreme Court has eight justices and one chief justice. John Roberts (seated, center) is the chief justice.

Each state has its own court system. Cities and towns have courts, too. Some courts deal with crimes. Crimes are acts that break the law. Other courts handle private problems. These problems are between people or between people and companies.

Some courts hold **trials.** During some trials, a group of people called the **jury** listens to the facts. They decide whether someone broke the law. At other trials, the judge makes the decision. If a person is found guilty, the judge usually decides what the punishment will be.

During a trial, the judge (center) listens closely as questions are being asked.

Leaders in all parts of government have important roles. The president serves more than 300 million people. Leaders of some towns serve fewer than 100 people. Their jobs may be different, but all leaders help keep our country strong.

In September 2005, President Bush met with Ray Nagin. He is the mayor of New Orleans, Louisiana. They worked on a plan to repair the city after Hurricane Katrina.

Glossary

bill: a written plan for a new law

budget: a plan for how to spend and make money

council: a group of people who are elected to make decisions for a city or town

elect: to choose a leader by voting

governor: the head of a state government

jury: a small group of people who decide during a trial whether someone has broken the law

legislature: the part of a government that makes the laws

mayor: the head of a city or town government

military: a country's armed forces

representative: a member of the House of Representatives, one of the two parts of Congress

senator: a member of the Senate, one of the two parts of Congress

trial: the official process of deciding in a court of law whether someone did something wrong

To Find Out More

Books

Hail to the Chief: The American Presidency. Don Robb (Charlesbridge)

Mayors. Shannon Knudsen (Lerner Publications)

The State Governor. First Facts: Our Government (series).
Mary Firestone (Capstone Press)

Web Sites
Inside the Courtroom
www.usdoj.gov/usao/eousa/kidspage/index.html
This site describes what goes on during a trial.

Kids in the House
clerkkids.house.gov
This site includes helpful information and fun activities about
Congress and the House of Representatives.

President for a Day
pbskids.org/democracy/presforaday/index.html
This site lets you become the president and plan your busy schedule.

Publisher's note to educators and parents: Our editors have carefully reviewed
these web sites to ensure that they are suitable for children. Many web sites
change frequently, however, and we cannot guarantee that a site's future
contents will continue to meet our high standards of quality and educational
value. Be advised that children should be closely supervised whenever they
access the Internet.

Index

About the Author

Jacqueline Laks Gorman grew up in New York City. She attended Barnard College and Columbia University, where she received a master's degree in American history. She has worked on many kinds of books and has written several series for children and young adults. She now lives in DeKalb, Illinois, with her husband, David, and children, Colin and Caitlin. She registered to vote when she turned eighteen and votes in every election.